Women in Conservation

Rachel Carson
Environmental Pioneer

Lori Hile

Heinemann
LIBRARY
Chicago, Illinois

Edited by Clare Lewis, Abby Colich, Diyan Leake, and Gina Kammer
Designed by Philippa Jenkins
Original illustrations © Capstone Global Library Ltd 2014
Illustrated by Oxford Designers and Illustrators
Picture research by Tracy Cummins
Production by Victoria Fitzgerald
Originated by Capstone Global Library Ltd
Printed and bound in China by CTPS

Library of Congress Cataloging-in-Publication Data
Hile, Lori
Rachel Carson: Environmental Pioneer
(Women in Conservation)

ISBN 978-1-4846-0471-7 (hardcover)
ISBN 978-1-4846-0476-2 (paperback)
ISBN 978-1-4846-0486-1 (eBook PDF)

18 17 16 15
10 9 8 7 6 5 4 3 2

Acknowledgments
We would like to thank the following for permission to reproduce photographs: Alamy: © Igor Golovnov, 40, © Jeff Rotman, 25; Corbis: © Bettmann, 30, 31, © Blue Lantern Studio, 8, © Pittsburgh Post-Gazette, 37; Getty Images: Alfred Eisenstaedt/Time Life Picture, 4, front cover, CBS Photo Archive, 36, JANEK SKARZYNSKI/AFP, 42, Nancy Honeycutt, 17, Roy Toft, 39; Indiana Historical Society: P0391, 9; Linda Lear Center for Special Collections & Archives, Connecticut College: 6, 7, 10, 11, 12, 13, 14, 21, Bob Hines, 27, Brooks Studios, 26, Edwin Gray, 24, Mary Frye, 16, Rex Gary Schmidt, 29, Shirley Briggs, 23; National Geographic: JAMES P. BLAIR, 33; Newscom: Everett Collection, 38, 43; Shutterstock: Jorge Salcedo, design element, Lone Wolf Photos, 19, neelsky, 41

We would like to thank Michael Bright and Linda Lear for their invaluable help in the preparation of this book.

Every effort has been made to contact copyright holders of any material reproduced in this book. Any omissions will be rectified in subsequent printings if notice is given to the publisher.

All the Internet addresses (URLs) given in this book were valid at the time of going to press. However, due to the dynamic nature of the Internet, some addresses may have changed, or sites may have changed or ceased to exist since publication. While the author and publisher regret any inconvenience this may cause readers, no responsibility for any such changes can be accepted by either the author or the publisher.

Contents

Some words are printed in bold, **like this**. You can find out what they mean by looking in the glossary on page 45.

Who Was Rachel Carson?

From the time she was a little girl, Rachel Carson wanted to be an author. She also loved exploring the natural world. After college, Carson combined these two passions. She wrote books and articles that introduced readers to the oceans and all the creatures that depend upon them. And she asked readers to help preserve and protect oceans and ocean life from **pollution**.

Even after Rachel Carson became a famous author and scientist, she felt most at home in nature.

But it was Carson's final book that made the biggest impact on the way people thought about the natural world. The book was called *Silent Spring*. In it, Carson asked readers to imagine the sounds of a spring morning without the rustle of rabbits, the buzz of bees, or the twitter of songbirds. She warned that this could happen. Human-made poisons called **pesticides** were leaking into the earth and killing birds, foxes, and other wildlife. Because we depend on nature, Carson believed humans could also be harmed. Her book alerted the public to a critical problem. It also helped inspire the environmental movement.

An unlikely crusader

Carson seemed like an unlikely crusader. She was reserved, soft-spoken, and shy. She felt more comfortable behind her writing desk or wading in tide pools than giving presentations or interviews. But Carson was a trained scientist with a deep love of nature. And she had a gift for making even the most complicated scientific information understandable to readers.

So, when she learned that there was a problem that could harm the natural world, Carson could not remain silent. This is her remarkable story.

In her own words

Explaining her decision to become a public figure, Carson said:

"Knowing the facts as I did, I could not rest until I had brought them to public attention."

How Did Carson Spend Her Childhood?

Carson grew up surrounded by nature in an old farmhouse near Springdale, Pennsylvania. A type of mining called strip mining would later **pollute** the air and water in this small village about 15 miles (24 kilometers) from Pittsburgh. But during Rachel's childhood, the Carsons' 64-acre (26-hectare) farm was a natural paradise, surrounded by woodlands and streams.

Growing up in nature

Rachel was the third child in her family. However, she sometimes felt like an only child. Her sister, Marian, was already 10 years old, and her brother, Robert, was eight when she was born in 1907.

Rachel (from left), Marian, and Robert ride a horse at their family home in Springdale, Pennsylvania.

Rachel often felt more at home with animals than with human companions.

While Rachel's siblings were at school, her mother, Maria, often took Rachel on nature walks into the woods and streams. A bird-watcher and former teacher, Maria created games to teach Rachel the names of birds, animals, and flowers. Rachel said she was "happiest with wild birds and creatures as companions." Her dog, Candy, followed her everywhere.

When Robert returned from school, he sometimes shot rabbits and squirrels for dinner, something Rachel always hated. Rachel took after her mother, who refused to even kill spiders that entered their house.

Although Rachel lived far from the ocean, she was always drawn to the idea of the sea.

In her own words

Rachel said of her childhood:

"I was rather a solitary child and spent a good deal of time in the woods and beside streams, learning the birds and the insects and the flowers."

DID YOU KNOW?

Fossils can reveal the history of a landscape. Rachel once found a fish fossil behind her home, 300 miles (483 kilometers) from the Atlantic Ocean. She later learned that a shallow sea once covered that area.

A budding author

Rachel's first love was nature, but she also delighted in reading and writing stories. Her mother read to her often and taught her how to read before she started school. Among Rachel's favorite books were *The Wind in the Willows* (1908) by Kenneth Grahame and Beatrix Potter's stories, with their lively animal characters.

Rachel's first stories were published in *St. Nicholas*, a popular children's magazine. The magazine also published stories by future authors William Faulkner, F. Scott Fitzgerald, E. E. Cummings, Edna St. Vincent Millay, and E. B. White.

ST NICHOLAS

JANUARY 1918

Gene Stratton-Porter

Indiana's Limberlost swamp inspired many of Gene Stratton-Porter's stories, novels, essays, photographs, and movies.

Gene Stratton-Porter

Rachel admired Gene Stratton-Porter, an American wildlife photographer and author best known for her novel *Girl of the Limberlost* (1909). Porter was also one of the first women to form her own movie production company in the 1920s. She used her fame and book income to help preserve **wetland** areas in Indiana, where she was from.

When Rachel was eight, Marian got married and left home. Robert joined the U.S. Air Force to fight in World War I (1914–1918). Often alone, Rachel began writing and designing covers for her own little books about plants and animals. She also entered a writing contest for the popular children's magazine *St. Nicholas*. Before she turned 11, her stories had won three top prizes. The magazine also bought an essay she wrote.

But Rachel's family had little money. Her father, Robert Sr., cobbled together a meager living working for the West Penn power plant and selling fruit from their orchards. To add income, Maria gave piano lessons. She always taught Rachel that nature, education, and self-worth were more important than expensive clothes or social status.

Top of the class

Rachel excelled at school, even though her mother sometimes kept her home, afraid she would catch contagious diseases. Despite her absences, Rachel ended up graduating at the top of her class.

Rachel's family lived far from her high school, which made visiting classmates difficult and expensive. Because of the distance and her quiet personality, Rachel had few friends. Yet Rachel's classmates respected her intelligence and hard work. They included this short poem next to Rachel's yearbook photo:

> Rachel's like the mid-day sun
> Always very bright
> Never stops her studying
> 'til she gets it right.

In her own words

Rachel recognized her mother's influence, saying:

"I can remember no time when I didn't assume I was going to be a writer. Also, I can remember no time when I wasn't interested in ... the whole world of nature. Those interests, I know, I inherited from my mother and have always shared with her."

Living far from town, Rachel spent more time with her dogs than her high school classmates.

Rachel's mother, Maria (pictured here in the 1880s), would live with Rachel and remain close to her the rest of her life.

At the time, most women got married or started working right after high school. But Rachel was determined to attend college. She was accepted to the Pennsylvania College for Women in nearby Pittsburgh. There she was awarded a **scholarship** to pay the expensive tuition. Her mother sold the family's good dishes to pay Rachel's room and board fees.

Maria Carson

Rachel's mother, Maria, was probably her biggest influence. Maria Carson was an accomplished singer, pianist, and student who graduated with honors in Latin before becoming a teacher. She quit teaching when she married because married women were not allowed to teach. But she was determined to pass on her love of books and nature to her children.

How Did College Inspire Carson?

When Rachel Carson started college in 1925, she planned to become a writer. By the end of her freshman year, she had written three pieces that her English professor, Grace Croft, singled out for praise. All of them demonstrated Carson's knowledge and love of nature. Her teacher especially praised Carson's ability to make technical concepts understandable—a skill that would serve her well in the future. Carson joined the staff of the school newspaper and *Englicode*, the school's literary magazine, which published many of her stories.

Outside of class, Carson was quiet and studious. She lacked the money and sophistication to participate in many campus social events. She did, however, join the field hockey and basketball teams and played with great enthusiasm, if not skill. Every weekend, she visited her parents in Springdale or hosted them at school.

Rachel stood out academically at Pennsylvania College for Women, but she did not share the wealth or social status many of her classmates enjoyed.

A popular teacher, Mary Scott Skinker encouraged her female students in science. This was met with disapproval by the college headmistress, which led to Skinker's eventual resignation (quitting her job).

Mary Scott Skinker

Carson's biology professor, Mary Scott Skinker, was an inspiration and role model for Carson. She had studied science at top universities at a time when women were believed to lack the seriousness needed to become scientists. Eager to share her knowledge, Skinker warmly encouraged her students. Skinker never lacked admirers, but she also never married. At the time, married women were expected to give up their careers, something Skinker was unwilling to sacrifice.

Rediscovering a passion

As a sophomore, Carson took a class in **biology**, which reawakened her early interest in plant and animal life. Her young teacher, Mary Scott Skinker, often took her students on field trips to local rock quarries, pools, and creeks. There, Carson learned to carefully observe the world around her.

A major decision

Grace Croft continued to praise Carson's stories and essays. Still, Carson worried that she lacked the imagination needed to be a writer. Instead, she started devoting more of her energy to biology, which combined her love of nature with her strong observational skills.

Carson, pictured in 1928, crammed most of her biology courses into her final year of college.

She considered changing her major from English to biology, a drastic step for women at the time. Writing and teaching were seen as suitable careers for women, but science was not. Female scientists could rarely find jobs, even as teachers.

The call of biology

One stormy night, as she considered her decision, Carson read a poem by the English poet Alfred Lord Tennyson called "Locksley Hall." The last line—"For the mighty wind arises, roaring seaward, and I go"—struck her like a bolt of lightning. She decided to follow the call of biology, feeling it might someday lead her to the sea.

Carson's decision to major in biology was met with disbelief and disapproval among many of her teachers and classmates. Even Miss Skinker was shocked—though pleased. But Carson had never been happier. She graduated in 1929 with high honors in **zoology**, a branch of biology focusing on animal life. And she received a full scholarship to Johns Hopkins University to earn her **master's degree**. Her hometown newspaper announced Carson's success, noting that the scholarship was "an honor given to few women."

In her own words

Reflecting on the line of Tennyson's poetry, Carson said:

"That line spoke to something within me... that my own destiny was somehow linked to the sea."

Skinker left the college before Carson graduated. But she kept in touch with Carson for years, offering her encouragement and career advice.

To the sea!

The summer after her college graduation, Carson spent six weeks doing field work at Woods Hole **Marine** Biological Laboratory. This was an educational center off the Massachusetts coast. It was Carson's first opportunity to visit the sea! The coast provided a wonderful hands-on laboratory for her. For the first time, she saw sea creatures in their natural **habitats**, rather than in jars in a laboratory. She also spent long hours in the library, learning facts about the sea and other subjects that fascinated her.

At Woods Hole, many of Carson's teachers and nearly half of her classmates were female. This was very rare in the world of science.

Rachel's summer at Woods Hole Marine Biological Laboratory in 1929 was one of her fondest memories.

Carson found her classes at Johns Hopkins University difficult but exciting.

Starting a new path

Before pursuing her master's degree in the fall, Carson visited the U.S. Bureau of Fisheries in Washington, D.C. While there, she talked with a supervisor named Elmer Higgins about jobs in science. When Carson informed him that she wanted to be a scientist—not a science teacher—Higgins was surprised, but he was impressed with her determination.

When Carson moved to Baltimore, Maryland, to attend Johns Hopkins University, she brought her entire family with her. While in school, she supported her mother, brother, and nieces. She also helped care for her sister and father, who were both ill. Carson was one of only a few women in her program at the university. She worked hard to show her professors that she was as smart as any man.

How Did Carson's Writing Help Her Work in Science?

After Carson earned her master's degree in 1932, she taught at two universities and sold articles to local newspapers. But money was tight. It was the middle of a very bad economic period called the Great Depression, and salaries were low. When Carson's father died in 1935, the family could not even afford to hold a funeral for him.

"Romance Under Water"

Carson knew she needed a higher-paying job. So she took an exam for government workers. Then she visited Elmer Higgins, the man from the Bureau of Fisheries.

Higgins desperately needed someone to write a series of short radio programs about undersea life. The scientists on his staff had no idea how to make fish biology interesting for listeners. Although Higgins had never seen Carson's writing, he took a chance and hired her. Now that she had a part-time job, Carson moved her family to Silver Spring, Maryland.

Carson's task was to write 52 short, informational radio shows on marine life called "Romance Under Water." The job was perfect for Carson because it allowed her to combine her writing skills with her knowledge of biology. Higgins was thrilled with her work, and the radio broadcasts were successful.

In her own words

Carson recalled:

"Eventually it dawned on me that by becoming a biologist I had given myself something to write about."

Focusing on Chesapeake Bay

Carson used the research from her radio scripts to write newspaper articles about the importance of preserving and protecting a clean marine environment. Many of her articles focused on the rapidly declining number of fish in Maryland's Chesapeake Bay. Carson believed that dangerous fishing methods and industrial pollution were harming the fish.

Carson wrote about pollution in Maryland's Chesapeake Bay in a way that most people easily understood.

Blending poetry and science

In April 1936, Carson sat quietly in Elmer Higgins' office. She waited as he read the 11-page introduction she wrote for a government brochure on marine life. Carson discussed sea life with a blend of poetry and science. Her writing took the reader on an undersea journey, bringing sea creatures into vibrant life.

Higgins was quiet for a moment. Then, he said: "I don't think this will do. Better try again." In truth, he was so impressed with the essay that he thought it belonged in a literary magazine, not a government pamphlet. He suggested she send the piece to the *Atlantic*, an American magazine known for its high-quality writing.

DID YOU KNOW?

When Carson's articles and government pamphlets were published, her name was always listed as "R. L. Carson," not "Rachel Carson." Carson believed the public would take her scientific work more seriously if they thought the writer was a man.

But Carson was busy writing other articles and taking care of her family. Her sister, Marian, died of the lung infection called pneumonia in 1937. This left Carson to care for her nieces, ages 12 and 11.

Finding an audience

Eventually, Carson submitted her essay to the *Atlantic* in the hopes of earning extra income. Later that year, the *Atlantic* published the article, called "Undersea."

The article impressed an editor from the book company Simon and Schuster, who encouraged Carson to expand it into a book. The thought had never occurred to Carson. But she decided to do it, writing late at night after long days at the office. Carson described herself as both a "perfectionist" and a "slow writer," so it took her several years to complete the book.

Carson worked for the U.S. Bureau of Fisheries as a biologist and writer between 1936 and 1952. This was her 1944 staff portrait.

How Did Carson Become Famous?

In November 1941, Carson's first book, *Under the Sea Wind*, was published. She dedicated it to her mother and included a special thank you to Elmer Higgins, "who started it all."

To introduce readers to the ocean, Carson told the story from the point of view of shorebirds and sea creatures. Carson gave each featured creature a name and a personality, but she based their behaviors and environments on years of careful research and observation. As part of her research, Carson spent 10 days at a fisheries station in Woods Hole, Massachusetts. While there, she scribbled notes about different fish and birds.

Critics praised the book's blend of science and story. The book sold well for several weeks—until the United States entered World War II (1939–1945).

Success—and stress

Meanwhile, Carson's government career flourished. She received several promotions and produced a series of booklets called "**Conservation** in Action." These booklets introduced the public to the national wildlife refuge system, which provides safe places for animals to live. The brochures stressed the importance of preserving wildlife habitats, since all **species** depend upon these resources.

Yet Carson's health suffered. She often worked overtime, then stayed up late at night writing. She lost weight and often caught colds. In 1946 doctors found a **tumor** on her breast—although they quickly removed it and claimed it was not **cancerous**. During this period, Carson dreamed of becoming a full-time writer, but she worried she could not support her family this way.

In her own words

Carson once said:

"I know that if I could choose what seems to be the ideal existence, it would be just to live by writing. But I have done far too little to dare risk it."

Rachel Carson got ideas for articles from traveling. Here, she is looking for raptors (birds that hunt other animals) at Hawk Mountain Sanctuary in eastern Pennsylvania in 1945.

Making the ocean interesting

During World War II, the public was interested in stories of submarine battles. But the average person knew little about the sea itself. For her second book, Carson wanted to introduce readers to the ocean in a way that would educate and fascinate them.

The great undersea adventure

As research, Carson arranged for a "great undersea adventure" off the Florida coast. She wore an 84-pound (38-kilogram) metal diving helmet and added weights to her feet. She sank 15 feet (5 meters) into the ocean to get a close-up look at the undersea world. The water was murky and she saw few fish. But now she could rely on her own experience, instead of just her imagination, when writing about undersea life.

Carson is taking notes at Woods Hole Marine Biological labs in 1950.

Before Carson could board the *Albatross III* fishing vessel similar to this one on Georges Bank, she had to convince the sailors that a woman on board would not bring them bad luck. She brought her agent, Marie Rodell, so that she would not be alone with 50 men.

Her next adventure was a 10-day voyage to Georges Bank, a famous fishing area 200 miles (322 kilometers) east of Boston, Massachusetts. Carson needed to collect information about the fishing grounds for the government. But she also hoped to learn about sea **currents** and creatures for her book.

Day and night, the fishing vessel she was on clanked, thundered, and rumbled as it hauled in its nets. These nets were bulging with fish, crabs, sponges, starfish, mussels, scallops, and other exotic creatures. The noise often kept Carson awake, but she was thrilled to examine the treasures piled in the fishermen's nets. She also learned about the ocean's makeup by watching a tool on the ship called a depth recorder. The recorder dangled underwater and traced the peaks and valleys of the ocean floor.

Inspired by her voyages, Carson began writing the book *The Sea around Us.* She poetically described places and sea creatures, using her own observations and the latest scientific information. She also consulted more than 1,000 publications and ocean experts around the world.

The Sea around Us

Carson started receiving fan mail even before *The Sea around Us* was published, after the *New Yorker* magazine printed parts of the book. Carson also received a check from the *New Yorker* for more money than she made in an entire year at her government job!

When *The Sea around Us* was published in 1951, it was an instant success. Critics loved the book, and it quickly climbed the best-seller charts. The book sold more than 250,000 copies the first year alone and won the National Book Award, a top literary prize.

Now that Carson was a popular author, she was often asked to give lectures, which made her nervous. But after a successful first speech, she gained confidence. She was still uncomfortable when fans approached her at the beauty salon or at her motel room door, seeking an autograph.

Rachel studies tiny living things under her microscope in 1951, the year *The Sea around Us* was published.

Rachel on the deck of Silverledges in 1960. Just seven years after her visit to the Maine coast, Rachel's dream of owning a home there became a reality.

To cash in on her popularity, Carson's publisher reprinted her first book, *Under the Sea Wind*. This too became a best seller and a critical success. Carson already had a third book in mind: a guide to undersea creatures and their habitats.

Silverledges

With two successful books, Carson finally had enough money to quit her government job and become a full-time writer. She could also realize her dream of building a summer cottage on the Maine shoreline.

Carson moved into a cottage she called Silverledges in June 1953, with her mother, her niece Marjie, and Marjie's son, Roger. At Silverledges, she quickly became friends with the Freemans, her new neighbors. Dorothy Freeman and Carson shared a love for cats and the seashore, and both were taking care of their elderly mothers.

Respect the protoplasm

Carson loved living by the water. There, she found the setting ideal for researching her next book. She wanted the book to show how different ocean environments —rocky shores, tide pools, and currents— attracted different kinds of sea creatures.

As part of this project, she wanted readers to consider the existence of tiny fish, bugs, and "a transparent wisp of a **protoplasm**" amid the rocky shores. She believed that wondering about these tiny things is a way of thinking about the mystery of life itself. While humans may not know the purpose of all creatures, Carson noted that all living things are part of an **ecosystem**. They depend on each other for survival. When one being is disturbed, so are all the beings in its ecosystem. Carson wanted readers to understand that humans, too, are part of the ecosystem.

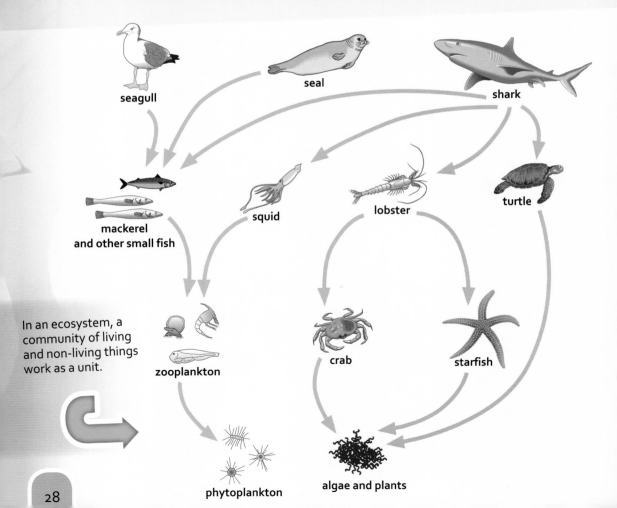

seagull

seal

shark

mackerel and other small fish

squid

lobster

turtle

In an ecosystem, a community of living and non-living things work as a unit.

zooplankton

crab

starfish

phytoplankton

algae and plants

28

Together, Rachel Carson and artist Bob Hines searched for fascinating sea creatures. While Rachel painted them with words, Bob painted them with a brush.

Creating *The Edge of the Sea*

After World War II, Carson realized how much human actions could affect the environment—for good or bad. As humans built bombs or bigger cities, she felt that people forgot their connection with nature. Since there is much that humans do not understand about nature's purpose, she wanted to encourage people to protect, rather than destroy, nature.

Carson chose Bob Hines, an artist at the U.S. Fisheries Bureau, to draw pictures of sea creatures for her new book. Together, they waded into the cold waters off the Maine coast—so cold, he sometimes had to carry her out! There, they examined fascinating sea life. *The Edge of the Sea* was published in 1955 to great acclaim.

How Did Carson Warn the Public About Pesticides?

In January 1958, Carson received sad news in a letter from her friend Olga Huckins. Huckins, who owned a bird sanctuary (safe haven) in Duxbury, Massachusetts, had found dozens of birds dead on her lawn. This happened the morning after officials had sprayed the area with a poisonous chemical called **DDT**. This "harmless shower" of pesticides was intended to kill mosquitos. But Huckins told Carson that the mosquitos were just as strong as ever.

Investigating DDT

Carson decided to investigate. From her work as an informational specialist for the Bureau of Fisheries, Carson knew that DDT had been used widely during World War II to protect troops against diseases spread by insects. Few tests were done on its safety. But this did not stop chemical companies from producing DDT and selling it to farmers and the general public to fight a "war on insects."

What is DDT?

DDT (dichlorodiphenyltrichloroethane) is a colorless, tasteless, and nearly odorless chemical compound. It harms living things by dissolving into the protective membrane, or skin, of cells (the tiny building blocks of life). This causes the minerals potassium and sodium to leak out of the cells. Without these minerals, living things suffer from uncontrollable movements of muscles called spasms or paralysis (not being able to move).

During the 1940s and 1950s, "fog machines" like this one regularly blanketed public areas with DDT, in an attempt to control insect pests.

Swiss scientist Paul Müller discovered DDT's ability to effectively kill insect pests in 1938. Müller later won a Nobel Prize for his discovery.

Yet by 1958, the negative side effects of DDT were becoming clear. Carson talked to experts all around the world. They described how birds, **beneficial insects**, and other wildlife were dying after "showers" of DDT were sprayed.

Carson soon realized there was enough information for a book. And since she knew more about the subject than just about anyone, she decided to write it.

In her own words

Carson once said:

"Man is a part of nature, and his war against nature is inevitably a war against himself."

A sad, slow start

Carson started researching DDT in 1958. She expected to complete the book a year later, but several unfortunate events slowed her progress. Between 1957 and 1958, both Carson's favorite niece, Marjie, and her own mother died of pneumonia. This left Carson the sole caretaker for Marjie's five-year-old son, Roger.

Then Carson discovered that she too was sick. The tumor that doctors had removed from Carson's breast years before had been malignant (cancerous) after all. And now the **cancer** was spreading. Carson underwent **radiation therapy** to help destroy it. Although the radiation treatments weakened her, she continued working.

Carson's research was also slow and painstaking. She talked with every scientist in North America and Europe who knew anything about pesticides. She also studied government reports and gathered large stacks of data.

DID YOU KNOW?
DDT saved thousands of lives when it was first used to kill mosquitos that spread a deadly disease called **malaria**.

Dangers of DDT

Carson would use her book to explain how the overuse of DDT can have disastrous effects on plants, soil, wildlife, and water. As she wrote the book, she gave examples of sick and dying birds. She also cautioned that the damage would only get worse, since every time a creature is exposed to DDT, the poison builds up in the body.

Carson also noted that DDT had affected wildlife in almost every region on Earth. Even birds in Antarctica were discovered with traces of DDT in their bodies.

DDT also hurt birds' abilities to have babies. Some chicks were born deformed, and some never hatched at all. Because of this, certain species of birds, including bald eagles, peregrine falcons, and brown pelicans, were near **extinction**.

Only one of twelve mallard ducks hatched from eggs affected by DDT.

A chain of destruction

Though insect pests were the targets of DDT, Carson explained how birds and other wildlife were often the unintentional victims.

First, the DDT poisoned leaves, seeds, and insects. Then, birds that ate these seeds were also poisoned. Then, foxes and other creatures that ate the poisoned birds began dying too, in a chain of destruction. And with fewer foxes left to kill rabbits, rabbits roamed free and destroyed farmers' crops—which was the very thing DDT was supposed to protect!

DDT also crept into the soil, water, and food supply, eventually reaching humans. Carson believed that DDT contributed to cancer in humans, although many scientists today dispute her claim.

fox

bird of prey

song bird

mouse

rabbit

Sprayed with DDT

worm

beetle

seeds

grass

leaves

The harmful effects of DDT rippled through the food chain from plants and insects to small animals, larger animals, and finally humans.

Nature fights back

Carson also found that DDT often failed in its goal of killing pests. At first, bugs would die. But, then the bugs began to produce stronger offspring (babies) that were resistant to (not affected by) pesticides. Soon, the bugs came back, stronger than ever.

Also, DDT destroys all bugs, even the ones that could keep pests at bay. For example, instead of just killing mosquitos, DDT also destroys ladybugs and praying mantises, which are bugs that could help kill mosquitos.

In Ontario, Canada, there were 17 times more black flies after DDT was sprayed. Why? Because their "enemy" bugs were killed by the poisons! This gave the black flies more plant and insect resources for themselves.

What Was the Reaction to *Silent Spring*?

Carson called her book about DDT *Silent Spring*. When it was published in September 1962, the public was stirred by Carson's poetic and passionate words, shocking examples, and stark facts. The book became a best seller. It inspired the public to question these "miracle chemicals" for the first time. In direct response to the book, U.S. President John F. Kennedy set up a committee to study the effects of pesticides.

Anger and outrage

But chemical companies, which made a great deal of money from selling pesticides, threatened to sue (take to court) Carson's publisher. When the publisher stood by Carson's facts, chemical companies called Carson unflattering names such as "**communist**" and "**spinster**." Some magazines and newspapers sided with the pesticide companies. They said her book contained oversimplifications and errors. And many people said that the death of wildlife was simply the price humans must pay for "progress."

In 1962 American news reporter Eric Sevareid interviewed Rachel Carson at her home in Silver Spring, Maryland, about the effects of pesticide use. The show aired on April 3, 1963.

The "gentle storm center"

In 1963 Carson appeared on a U.S. TV special, along with a pesticide company scientist. While Carson spoke calmly and knowledgeably about the problems pesticides posed, the man from the chemical company made exaggerated and scary statements. He said insects and diseases would take over the earth if Carson had her way.

If Carson had any doubters before the special, her careful and calm presence reassured them. *Life* magazine called her "the gentle storm center." But Carson's breast cancer was taking its toll. She was so weak during the filming that she had to prop her head on her hands.

In her own words

Carson responded to critics who said DDT was necessary to control insects. She said:

"I do not favor turning nature over to insects. I favor the sparing, selective and intelligent use of chemicals."

When *Silent Spring* was published, Rachel Carson was already a beloved best-selling author. Her popularity helped her survive attacks from critics and the chemical companies.

Taking a stand

Shortly after the TV special, Carson testified before President Kennedy's Science Advisory Committee. On May 15, 1963, the committee issued a report. It supported Carson's scientific claims and recommended a reduction in pesticide use.

A month later, Carson testified in front of a Senate subcommittee. She called for policies to protect human health and the environment. Sadly, by this time Carson was very sick. She wore a wig because her hair had fallen out from radiation therapy, and she had trouble walking. Yet, close friends said that her failing health made her even more determined to share her message.

Though sick at the time, Carson spoke forcefully to a Senate subcommittee in 1963 about the harmful effects of DDT on animals.

Life cycles

Carson quietly arranged for her editor to care for her nephew, Roger, after her death. And she spent time at her cabin in Maine, finding comfort in nature and talking with Dorothy Freeman. One day the two friends watched monarch butterflies as they migrated south. Later Carson wrote to Freeman about the experience. She said she found happiness in watching them, even knowing the butterflies would not live long enough to return. She accepted that all living things had a natural end to their life cycles.

On April 14, 1964, Carson died at her home in Silver Spring, Maryland. She was 56 years old. She had wanted a small ceremony, but her brother held her funeral at a big church. Several visitors noted that the signs in the church parking lot read: "No parking from 7 a.m.–4 p.m. Trees will be sprayed with pesticides." Fortunately, this type of mass spraying would soon become a thing of the past, thanks to Rachel Carson.

Carson took comfort in the natural life cycle of the monarch butterfly.

A springboard for environmental action

The ideas and information Carson introduced changed the way we think about the environment. Inspired by her work, many people took action to protect the environment and to conserve wildlife.

Just five months after Carson's death, in 1964, the U.S. Congress passed the Wilderness Act. This law protected 9 million acres (3.6 million hectares) of national forests in the United States. Three years later, in 1967, a group of American scientists documented the harmful effects of DDT on birds called raptors and osprey. They formed a group called the Environmental Defense Fund and successfully got DDT banned in New York.

Banning DDT

In 1970 a U.S. government agency called the Environmental Protection Agency (EPA) was created for the specific purpose of protecting human health and the environment. Together, the EPA and the Environmental Defense Fund helped get a law passed in 1972 that banned the sale of DDT in the United States.

In 1972 the first international conference on the environment was held in Stockholm, Sweden.

DID YOU KNOW?

DDT is still used in parts of South America, Africa, and Asia to kill insects that carry malaria and other diseases. It is also permitted in parts of North America and Europe for emergency disease control.

In 1981, 18 years after her death, the U.S. Postal Service issued a postage stamp honoring Rachel Carson.

Falcons take flight

At the time of Carson's death, peregrine falcons were facing extinction. DDT had hurt their ability to reproduce (have babies). After DDT was restricted in 1972, scientists worked to save the species by raising chicks in cages. In 1979 three healthy young falcons were released into the wild. One of the falcons was named Rachel.

Once endangered by exposure to DDT, peregrine falcons recovered after DDT was banned and the birds' nesting places were protected.

What Is Carson's Legacy?

Rachel Carson accomplished much in her short life. She was the first person to explain to the public how human-made poisons affect every part of our environment. She showed us that nature is interconnected and that humans must consider these connections when making decisions.

Many of today's environmental issues have their roots in these lessons from Carson. **Climate change**—the theory that human actions affect our planet's climate—is a direct result of Carson's ideas. Carson's nephew, Roger, believes if his great aunt were alive today, she would be leading the cause to solve climate change. Climate change affects the oceans and the species that depend on them.

Silent Spring had a "profound influence" on climate change activist (and former U.S. vice president) Al Gore. He has called the book "a cry in the wilderness that changed history." He has said, "Without it, the environmental movement ... might never have happened at all."

Influenced by Rachel Carson, climate change activist Al Gore won the Nobel Peace Prize in 2007 for his efforts to combat climate change.

Much work has been completed since *Silent Spring*, but there is still more work to do.

Work to be done

There is still work to be done on environmental issues. Pesticides are still used, and some are much more powerful than DDT. Untested or unsafe chemicals are also found in everyday items, including plastic containers, electronic equipment, and household cleaners. And industries continue to pollute the air, land, and water. Yet, now there is more than one voice speaking out. Thanks to Carson, there is a whole chorus of people working together. The environmental movement will only grow larger and more powerful if dedicated individuals continue to learn about these issues and fight for them, as Rachel Carson did.

In her own words

Carson once said:

"Conservation is a cause that has no end. There is no point at which we will say, 'our work is finished.'"

Timeline

1907 Rachel Carson is born in Springdale, Pennsylvania, on May 27

1917 Carson publishes her first story, at age 10, in *St. Nicholas* magazine

1925 Graduates from high school at the top of her class

1929 Graduates from college with high honors in zoology; visits the sea for the first time during a summer course at the Marine Biological Laboratory in Woods Hole, Massachusetts

1932 In June, Carson earns a master's degree in zoology from Johns Hopkins University

1935 Carson's father dies, leaving Rachel the sole supporter for her family. After, Carson begins to write for the U.S. Bureau of Fisheries and also writes newspaper articles

1937 The *Atlantic* magazine publishes Carson's essay "Undersea." Carson's sister, Marian, dies, leaving Carson to care for two nieces

1941 Carson's first book, *Under the Sea Wind*, is published

1946 Doctors remove a tumor from Carson's breast, but they believe it is not cancerous

1951 Carson's second book, *The Sea around Us*, is published

1952 Carson gives up her job at the Bureau of Fisheries to focus full time on her writing

1953 Moves into her summer home in Southport Island, Maine

1955 Carson's third book, *The Edge of the Sea*, is published

1957 Carson's niece Marjie dies, leaving Carson to care for Marjie's five-year-old son

1958 Carson's mother, Maria, dies

1960 Carson discovers that she has cancer

1962 *Silent Spring* is published

1963 *April 3*: Carson appears on the U.S. television special "The Silent Spring of Rachel Carson," where she wins viewers over with her calm, steady, and informed presence

May 15: The Science Advisory Committee issues a report, supporting Carson's scientific claims

June 3: Carson testifies about the use of pesticides before a Senate subcommittee

1964 On April 14, Carson dies in her home in Silver Spring, Maryland

1970 The Environmental Protection Agency (EPA) is created in the United States to protect human health and the environment

1972 The sale of DDT is banned in the United States, although it can still be exported (sent) to other nations

1980 Carson is posthumously (after her death) awarded the Presidential Medal of Freedom by U.S. President Jimmy Carter

1991 The Rachel Carson Prize, an international award honoring women for outstanding achievements in environmental issues, is established in Stavanger, Norway

2004 The Audubon Society establishes the Rachel Carson Award, honoring women who have helped the environmental movement

2007 Al Gore, whose ideas were inspired by Carson, wins a Nobel Peace Prize for his work on climate change

Glossary

beneficial insect types of insect that perform services humans consider valuable, such as killing insects that harm crops, plants, or humans

biology science of life or living matter

cancer disease in which cells in the body grow too fast and can clump together to form a tumor

cancerous related to the disease cancer

climate change theory that human actions affect our planet's climate

communist person who believes in the principles of communism, which supports a society in which all property belongs to the community, rather than private owners

conservation protection and care of an animal or place

current body of water or air moving in a specific direction

DDT a colorless compound primarily used to kill insects; short for "dichlorodiphenyltrichloroethane"

ecosystem complex set of relationships among organisms (living things) and their environment; it includes plants, trees, animals, fish, birds, microorganisms, water, soil, and people

extinction state of being dead; no longer existing

fossil remains or impression of a living thing from long ago

habitat natural home or environment of an animal, plant, or other living thing

malaria serious disease that causes chills and fever and that is passed from one person to another by the bite of mosquitoes

marine relating to the sea or found in the sea

master's degree diploma awarded by a graduate school to a student who has completed at least one year of study beyond college

pesticide substance used to kill pests, especially insects that damage or interfere with the growth of crops, shrubs, or trees

pollute make air, water, or earth dirty or harmful to people, plants, and animals by adding harmful chemicals or waste

pollution presence of a substance or substances that are harmful or poisonous

protoplasm living contents of a cell; the liquid substance of a cell

radiation therapy type of cancer treatment that uses beams of energy to kill cancer cells

scholarship amount of money that is given by a school or organization to a student to help pay for the student's education

species group of living things that are related to each other

spinster old-fashioned and negative word for a woman who has never been married and is beyond the age at which women traditionally marry

terminal nerve any of the network of nerve strands passing to the nose and carrying odor sensations to the brain

tumor abnormal growth of body tissue; tumors can be cancerous (malignant) or noncancerous (benign)

wetland wet lowland area, such as a marsh, swamp, or bog, that is considered the natural habitat of wildlife

zoology branch of science that involves the study of animals and animal behavior

Find Out More

Books

Ehrlich, Amy. *Rachel: The Story of Rachel Carson*. San Diego: Harcourt, 2003.

Landau, Elaine. *Rachel Carson and the Environmental Movement* (Cornerstones of Freedom). New York: Children's Press, 2004.

Lawlor, Laurie. *Rachel Carson and Her Book That Changed the World*. New York: Holiday House, 2012.

Levine, Ellen. *Rachel Carson: A Twentieth-Century Life* (Up Close). New York: Viking, 2007.

Quaratiello, Arlene Rodda. *Rachel Carson: A Biography*. Amherst, N.Y.: Prometheus Books, 2010.

Websites

www.fws.gov/rachelcarson/
Learn more about Carson from videos, photos, and other resources. This web site was created by the U.S. government's Fish and Wildlife Service, the organization where Carson worked for many years.

www.kidsplanet.org
Learn how to defend, protect, and enjoy wildlife through activities, resources, games, and facts about different animal species.

www.rachelcarsoncouncil.org
This web site informs the public about the effects of pesticides and offers some alternative ways to manage pests. Click on "kids activities" to find a Rachel Carson biography, trivia questions, activities, and ways you can help the environment.

www.rachelcarson.org
Find a timeline, research guide, and brief biography of Carson.

DVDs

American Experience: Rachel Carson's Silent Spring. Boston: WGBH Boston Video, 2007.

A Sense of Wonder: Two Interviews with Rachel Carson. Oley, Pa.: Bullfrog, 2009.

Bill Moyers Journal: Rachel Carson, Nature's Guardian. Princeton, N.J.: Films for the Humanities and Sciences, 2007.

Places to Visit

The Rachel Carson National Wildlife Refuge

York and Cumberland counties, Maine
www.fws.gov/refuge/rachel_carson/
Along Carson's beloved coast of Maine, the Rachel Carson National Wildlife Refuge was established in 1966 to protect salt marshes for birds. Visitors can fish, hunt, kayak and canoe, search for shellfish, and view thousands of plants and animals unique to the region, including salt marsh sparrows and other wading birds.

Rachel Carson Reserve

Southern Carteret county, North Carolina
www.nccoastalreserve.net/web/crp/rachel-carson
Rachel Carson encouraged people to protect natural places and wild creatures. You can see her work in action at the Rachel Carson Reserve, an island off the North Carolina coast that is home to a herd of wild horses. More than 200 species of birds have also been observed at the site, including 23 rare or endangered species. Visitors must take a private boat or ferry to reach the island.

The Rachel Carson Homestead

613 Marion Avenue
Springdale, Pennsylvania 15144
http://rachel_carson_homestead.myupsite.com
If you would like to see where Carson grew up, you can visit the Rachel Carson Homestead, a small, five-room farmhouse in Springdale, Pennsylvania, overlooking the Allegheny River.

Your own backyard or nearby park

Sometimes we forget to stop and observe the insects, birds, bird nests, and small creatures all around us.

What can I do?

There are things you can do every day to help protect our planet, such as:

- Ask your family to buy "pesticide-free" or organic foods (foods produced without the use of pesticides or chemical additives).

- Ask your family not to use pesticides in your home or garden. These can be dangerous for children and pets.

- Stop using plastic. Plastic wraps, containers, and water bottles are polluting our oceans. Many plastic water and soda bottles are also made with chemicals that can be dangerous for humans. Recycle plastic bags and bottles. Choose paper over plastic. Use refillable water bottles.

- You can save 25 gallons (95 liters) of water each month if you simply turn off the water while brushing your teeth!

- Start a recycling club at your school and pick up litter.

- Write a letter to a member of Congress asking for stronger pesticide laws.

Index